The Banana Spider

by Anne Giulieri

Let's look at a *banana* spider!

A banana spider

is big and hairy.

Banana spiders have 8 *legs*.

Banana spiders have 8 *eyes*.

A banana spider
is a long spider.

Let's look at a banana spider!

Here are a banana spider's:

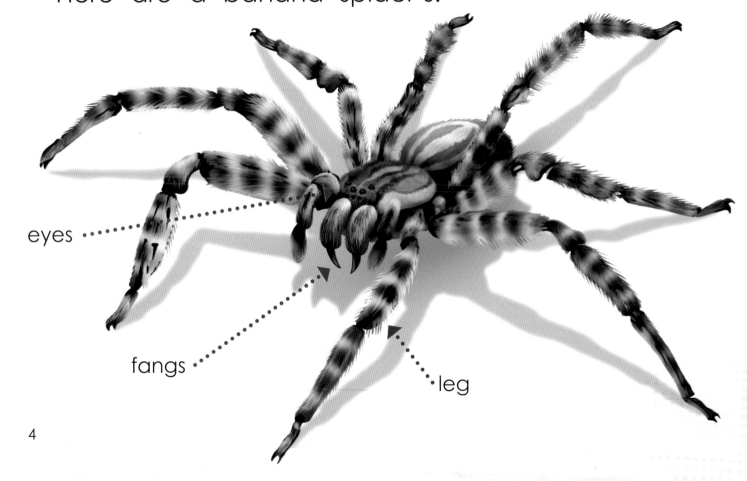

eyes

fangs

leg

A banana spider has two big *fangs*
and long hairy legs.

Let's look at spiders!

This is a *crab* spider
but it is not like a crab!

This is a *wolf* spider
but it is not like a wolf!

This is a banana spider
but it is not like a banana!

7

Let's look at the banana spider's name!

The banana spider is not a banana.

You cannot eat a banana spider.

The banana spider hides in bananas. Can you find it?

The banana spider likes to hide
in long banana *leaves*, too.
Can you find it?

Look! Can you see the banana spider
eating a little brown *lizard*?

Let's look at my banana spider!

It is big and brown.

It is hairy,

and it is very, very scary!

You can make

a banana spider, too.

Picture Glossary

banana

fangs

lizard

crab

leaves

wolf

eyes

legs

Banana spiders come
from South America.

16